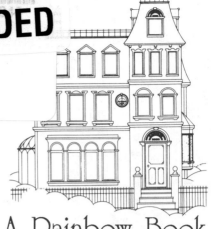

A Rainbow Book

HOW TO AVOID PATENT, MARKETING & INVENTION COMPANY SCAMS

HOW TO AVOID PATENT, MARKETING & INVENTION COMPANY SCAMS

Wow! What a Great Idea . . . Now What?

Martin C. Smith,
Inventor

RAINBOW BOOKS, INC.

Library of Congress Card Cataloing in Publication Data

Smith, Martin C. (Martin Christopher), 1964-
   How to avoid patent, marketing & invention company scams : wow!
what a great idea . . . now what?   / Martin C. Smith.
      p.   cm.
   ISBN   1-56825-020-7   : $9.95
   1. Inventions — Marketing.   2. Patents.   3. Swindlers and
swindling.   I. Title.   II. Title: How to a avoid patent, marketing
and invention company scams.
   T339.S63   1995   94-37648
   608.773'068'6—dc20   CIP

Published by Rainbow Books, Inc.
P. O. Box 430, Highland City, FL 33846-0430.

HOW TO AVOID PATENT, MARKETING
& INVENTION COMPANY SCAMS
Wow! What a Great Idea . . . Now What?
by Martin C. Smith
Cover by Betsy Lampé
Interior Design by Marilyn Ratzlaff
$9.95
ISBN: 1-56825-020-7

DEDICATION

This book is dedicated . . .

To my loving wife, Tamra Dawn. Your inspiration and endless support made this and several other dreams a reality.

To my two sons, Brandon and Blake. Each and every day I feel inspired and extremely happy to be your father.

And finally to my uncle, Joe Graves. My memories of your thoughtfulness will survive.

CONTENTS

10

PREFACE

In a world economy, many people suffer from overwhelming expenses and too short of income. Many people, in fact, often wonder how wealth could change their lives. Well, if you are one of the millions with these dreams and have a new invention that you believe may bring you good fortune, then please read this book CAREFULLY to avoid wasting thousands and thousands of your hard-earned dollars introducing your idea to the market!

Obviously, if you have ever had a new product idea, you may dream of making a million bucks! Right? Truth is, many new product ideas never get patented, marketed or developed, because there are huge out-of-pocket expenses incurred by the inventor. However, there are many avenues of introducing a new product to market on a small fixed budget. These avenues are key processes for inventors with small budgets (mostly their own investment monies) that will yield a great return, depending on the invention's success.

These processes are only known through discovered secrets for introducing a successful product to market on a fixed budget. Inventor, don't get discouraged!

To avoid making costly investment errors in areas which may not produce any financial rewards, the author of this book provides a wealth of knowledge obtained by losing thousands and thousands of dollars to introduce a new product to market. This book will help inventors avoid the loss of money and the victimization of what can only be considered a nationwide SCAM.

To begin, a new product idea is the backbone of a free market society. The American society, fathered by our Constitution of the United States, has allowed many Americans to proceed from flat broke to unlimited wealth, using the ingenuity of the common consumer. Although the American system may be the best in the world (as noted by the changing economies in the world to free market systems and democracy type governments), there still remains a colossal beguilement that may affect every new product inventor or idea introduced to market. I call it, The Patent, Marketing and Invention Company SCAM.

Today, there are thousands of lawyers and companies/corporations that cater to individuals requiring assistance in introducing their new product idea to the market place. Although many patent attorneys, marketing companies and invention assistance companies may be honest and ethical businesses, based on this inventor's experience, I have found many to be nothing but a pit of deceit!

Inventor, please do be careful. Read every word of this book to avoid one of our greatest national SCAMS!

INTRODUCTION TO PATENTS

HISTORY OF PATENTS

The idea of protecting an individual's creativity has existed for hundreds of years. The first known patent was issued by the Republic of Florence in 1421. This patent granted only a small amount of protection for the inventor as compared to today's corporate product idea patents (Utility and Design). The patent was known of, but the legal requirements for the patent, were never established.

In 1471, fifty years later, an ordinance relating to patents was enacted in Venice. The ordinance resulted in an almost wide spread issue of "monopolies" for all European Countries. Although these monopolies existed, no legal statues, protecting the inventor, were developed until 1624.

In 1624, a Statute of Monopolies passed in the British Parliament that restricted granting of monopolies for anything other than new inventions. This action confirmed authority to grant exclusive rights for inventions for a term of fourteen years. This movement lead to development of patent legislation in the United States.

The first Patent Bill in the United States was enacted by the father of our country, George Washington, on April 10, 1790. The bill gave inventors the right to exclude all individuals from using, making and selling their invention.

The Patent Bill introduced and defined the subject matter of a patent as, "Any useful art, manufactured engine machine or device, or any improvement therein not before known or used." This Patent Bill established the first patent board under jurisdiction of the State Department.

The State Department's first approved patent, issued July 31, 1790, was granted to Samuel Hopkins of Pittsford, Vermont, for making potash and pearlash by a new apparatus and process. The State Department retained jurisdiction of all patents until 1849, when jurisdiction of the patenting process was transferred to the Department of Interior where it remains today.

Although the Department of Interior has made few changes to the patent laws of today, they did enact and change a patent's life from fourteen to seventeen year rights (a patent also may be extended past seventeen years by an act of Congress), depending on the type of patent. However, the life of a patent today may be shortened to only a few years, depending on the amount of money an inventor has for patent servicing.

Patent servicing, "an action of government to collect *royalties* from all inventors to keep an *inventor's* patent active," is a payment many inventors never realize, until after they have received a patent. These fees are costly and must be maintained to ensure the life of the patent. A more detailed explanation about costs of patent servicing will be outlined later.

Now that the short history lesson is over, I will explain costs associated with patenting in the 1990s and will detail a step-by-step outline at the end of each section for inventors to successfully introduce a new product to market. The step-by-step outline will help inventors avoid Patent, Market and Invention Company SCAMS.

Although many new inventors may have never experienced the possible SCAM, the author did realize the SCAM — but after it was in full effect. I fell victim to this significant problem. But by utilizing this book, all new inventors will successfully avoid the Patent, Market and Invention Company SCAM!

CHAPTER 1

PATENTS AND
THE PATENT SCAM

it later to rescind the attorney's request for payment.

The second option, creating the patent yourself, entails a time-consuming and painstaking process.

Although creating the patent yourself is frustrating, many individuals have saved thousands and thousands of dollars by creating their own patent. If the inventor chooses to create his/her own patent, your local library can help tremendously. There is an extensive collection on how to patent an idea yourself. Remember, be patient and consult the United States Patent and Trademark Office with direct and specific questions regarding your patent.

The third option in the patent process, not to patent your idea at all, is available to people who have an idea and choose not to spend time writing the patent or do not want to spend thousands of dollars patenting the concept. This option seeks the assistance of a large or small corporation for assistance and development of the idea.

Today, many corporations are looking for good ideas, and many inventors are looking to sell good ideas. Ah, yes, you can submit your idea to a large or small corporation for sale without a patent. That's right. Sell the idea WITHOUT a patent.

Although selling the idea without a patent is the best alternative for fixed budget entrepreneurs, you must still seek protection for your idea via a "Non-Disclosure" agreement. This is the least expensive, least time-consuming option but does not provide the *BEST* legal protection.

A "Non-Disclosure" agreement is a document usually containing written literature which informs the reviewing entities that the sole owner of an idea maintains all rights and privileges under stated laws. The reviewing entity may not disclose any information about the idea without written permission from the submitting party. Thus, the "Non-Disclosure" agreement will legally bind all reviewing parties and will avoid a potential entity from *stealing* your idea, once completed. The inventor also must not disclose any information about the idea to a company or individual until the signed "Non-Disclosure" agreement is initiated with the potential customer or company and re-

CHAPTER 1

PATENTS AND THE PATENT SCAM

TYPES OF PATENTS

Today patents come in various types with the most popular types being design and utility patents. To be patentable, the invention, design, or process must be genuine, useful, novel and not obvious in light of presently known technology.

As noted, there are three types of patents from which an inventor may select. The most popular is a utility patent, then a design patent, and lastly a plant filing.

The most popular type of patent, a utility patent, is intended to give rights to inventors for internal and external operating configurations. Also, the utility patent is subdivided into three major categories:

1. Device or Apparatus;
2. Method of operation of Apparatus
   (how device works);
3. Composition Claims
   (material composition protection).

This type of patent provides seventeen year rights and is subject to maintenance/service fees. Some examples of common utility patents may be a watch, video cassette recorder lock, or a Vide-O-Lock for Nintendo[1] Games.

---

[1]Nintendo is a registered trademark of Nintendo of America, Inc.

The second most popular type of patent is a design patent. Design patents provide exterior or external type protection with no provisions for internal or operating apparatus configurations. Design patents provide four-teen year protection and are not subject to maintenance/service fees. An example of a design patent may be the old style Coca-Cola glass bottles or IBM's outside shell for computers.

The third type of patent, a plant filing, provides protection for genetic type development. These patents are uniquely different from a design or utility patent. Please check with the United States Patent and Trade-mark office for regulations on plant filings. An example of a plant filing may be a new lime-green rose with purple polkadots. A sick thought, but appropriate.

These three patents listed above are the most common types of patents. There are other types of patents, but the inventor must determine which type is necessary, prior to proceeding with his/her patent. Please contact the United States Patent and Trademark Office or a spe-cialized patent book for assistance.

Author Recommendation

If I were to recommend a patent type, based on this inventor's experience, I would select a utility type patent. These patents are easily defined legible patents, stating basic intent of the idea and its uses. Additional informa-tion on types of appropriate patents for your product are available through your local library.

PATENT PROCESS

The process by which an inventor receives a patent is time consuming with the most time elapsing after an inventor submits his/her patent to the government for review. Although some individuals in poor health or other unusual circumstances may receive special attention from the patent review board, most inventors must wait six to eighteen months for a review of their patent.

Today a patent is useful to guarantee an individual's right to sole ownership. A patent may be granted for protection in the United States, or an inventor may select protection from other foreign countries by an issuance of a patent from said country.

A large portion of inventors fail to realize a United States patent is only good for the United States. If an inventor would like protection in Japan, Germany, etc., they must seek an international patent and pay substantially increased patent fees for each country.

Remember: A United States patent provides protection in the United States only. Don't be fooled by a patent attorney who fails to inform you of your limited protection and coverage.

The patent process usually begins with the inventor having only three options for a patentable idea. First, the inventor may seek assistance of a patent attorney to develop the patent; second, the inventor may attempt to create his/her own patent; and third, the inventor may opt to not patent the idea at all.

The first option in the patent process, selection of a GOOD patent attorney, usually involves finding an individual who has an extensive patent preparation background, is a trustworthy advisor, and is upfront about the numerous patent fees which may exist. These individuals are hard to find, and unfortunately the author failed to locate such an individual. (My attorney never informed me of the numerous patent fees.)

As an inventor, ask the attorney for a record of fees from the United States Patent and Trademark office. Discuss the type of patent which you have selected (design or utility) and ask the attorney to highlight fees from the United States Patent and Trademark office for which you will be responsible. Also, discuss what additional fees the attorney requires for his/her services. Please, for your safety, keep this highlight fee form on file; you may need

tained by the inventor for the inventor's records.

Many attorneys fail to enlighten inventors on the well-known "Non-Disclosure" form. These forms enable an individual with just an idea to submit the idea in good faith to a corporation or individual for purchase considerations. These forms are available in most patent attorney's offices and a copy is included in the back of this book.

To complete a "Non-Disclosure" form, simply locate the corporation or individual which you feel may have interest in your product idea (you may consult your local library for names of corporate officials, phone numbers and addresses). I recommend that you obtain the name of vice-president of marketing or vice-president of new product ideas to discuss the options of your idea.

Simply call or meet with the corporation or individual responsible for reviewing new product ideas. Discuss possibilities of submitting your idea for purchase consideration, but do be careful not to disclose your invention. Be very vague in discussions referring to your invention. Ask if you may send a "Non-Disclosure" form. They must sign the form and return it, prior to you disclosing information pertaining to the invention.

Author's Note

As added protection, you may choose to send your "Non-Disclosure" agreement certified restricted mail. Once you receive the signed "Non-Disclosure" form from the reviewing entity, keep this form in a safe place. This may be your only right of protection against a company or individual with whom you disclosed your information. You may now discuss openly your idea with *only* the individual who signed your disclosure agreement. Also, you may want to have witnesses sign a form stating that they have seen your idea, prior to submitting a disclosure form to the prospective buyers. Don't forget to make your witnesses sign a disclosure form also. You can't be too careful!

Now, with your "Non-Disclosure" agreement on file and your new product idea in the hands of a potential customer, you may be on your way to making millions from royalties with only the small investment of the price of this book. How easy. But remember to protect yourself from all possible pitfalls and idea pirates!

OPPORTUNITY COSTS

The three choices presented in this section, regarding the patenting process, all have opportunity costs. The first option of choosing a patent attorney usually results in large out-of-pocket fees, but it saves the inventor time required to write the patent.

The second option of writing the patent yourself may result in a lack of protection for the inventor because the claims could be misappropriated. It will, however, save the inventor thousands and thousands of dollars.

The third option of allowing a corporation or individual to develop the invention, may result in possible court battles to prove the idea submitted to a company was yours. But don't worry. Your disclosure agreement should help win the case. Also the third option could result in a company paying for all patent fees, manufacturing fees and marketing fees. This will save the inventor from the "Patent, Marketing and Invention Company's SCAM."

The choice is difficult, but a clear decision can easily be made. List the positive points of all choices and use some deductive reasoning. Then, you'll make the very best choice.

SUMMARY OF PATENTING AND
LESSONS LEARNED

There are many lessons in life which, unfortunately, are learned only by experience. To learn the lessons of patenting, you must have patented a product or idea previously, as did the author. Or you must learn from someone else's experiences.

The first error this inventor made was seeking the help of a patent attorney. Patent attorneys are not all crooks, but a majority of them, including the attorney I chose, may not disclose all potential elements in the patent process. As I mentioned earlier, this was an expensive mistake.

To avoid future mistakes for other inventors, I will disclose to you the good processes and bad mistakes for patenting a great idea. Here is my summary . . .

One night, while off in "Dream Land," the most impressive idea came to me. I dreamed of an inquisitive child spoon-feeding a video cassette recorder (VCR) with oatmeal. You may recall the television commercial? A device that would prevent this awful problem came to my mind.

Upon awakening the following morning, quickly the device was developed and engineered before the idea disappeared.

Proceeding with the process, with a lack of knowledge, a decision was made to seek a patent; after all, no one wants a great idea copied or stolen.

A patent attorney in Arizona was selected by advice of my colleagues, who all signed a "Non-Disclosure" agreement. I had learned of a "Non-Disclosure" agreement from a corporate patent attorney. Upon arriving in the patent attorney's office, immediately impressive and expensive furnishings appeared. Wow! This was the place to be. Riches and fortunes would soon follow.

Seeing the walls of this individual's office covered with numerous law degree certificates and business type licenses, immediately a somewhat comfortable feeling overcame me. This person obviously knew what he was doing. After all, the government doesn't allow attorneys to excessively charge clients, right?

The process began with a showing of detailed drawings and a prototype of the invention. Convincingly, the attorney assured me there probably was nothing else similar to the idea, but we must proceed by the book and perform a patent search. He informed me the search would cost around $600.00, but my idea was great and original, and no one else probably had already invented it. Thus, the attorney collected $600.00. (Attorney $600.00 — Author/me zero). As a point of interest, most colleges and universities offer a patent search for only the cost of computer time which totals roughly $75.00.

The attorney's search resulted in one or two similar ideas, but both ideas were designed to prevent people from inserting food and foreign material into cassette players. The attorney assured me my idea was patentable, and we must proceed at once with the process.

A couple of weeks had passed since the return of my patent search. The attorney informed me the cost of my patent was $2,250.00. This included all patent costs, according to the attorney. Also, this included the writing of all patent claims, abstracts and the patent filing fee of $365.00. This sounded reasonable. So, the attorney collected $2,250.00. (Attorney $2,850.00 — Author/me zero).

Upon completion of the patent, the attorney reviewed with me all claims and clauses pertaining to the invention. The stated claims seemed very vague. Indeed, the claims seemed to grant protection for everything ever developed on any electronic apparatus.

The attorney indicated the claims were "broad" but that was a normal practice in patent writing. Assuredly, the attorney said, "There's nothing to worry about, the claims are solid, the United States patent examiner will certainly allow for all claims. This is increased protection of your idea — having such broad claims."

This sounded reasonable, but the question still remained: Would the United States Patent and Trademark office accept the patent?

The process for a patent review by the United States Patent and Trademark office was time consuming. Approximately six months had passed and still no reply. Finally, a reply was sent to my attorney's office. The United States Patent and Trademark office had rejected all claims. Further, the attorney stated in a written letter that for him to address all the United States patent examiner's concerns, an additional $750.00 fee was needed.

What! Instantly, my blood pressure soared. Thoughts of additional money to patent my idea caused my stomach to knot like a fist. But not to worry. I pulled myself together, and a meeting was set to discuss problems and the attorney's request for additional payment. Obviously, we had misunderstood communication. The attorney had quoted me $2,250.00 to write my patent.

The attorney quickly pointed out the claims were all approved by me, and he had tried his "damndest" to get the patent approved. To fix my patent, he needed an additional $750.00.

But what about the $2,250.00 given to him initially, and the $600.00 for the search?

The attorney replied, "That doesn't cover changes to the patent and my additional time to review the examiner's concerns."

Again, the question was presented to the attorney, Why didn't you tell me this could happen?

The attorney replied, "Because all patents are different, and most get approved the first time."

Aye, right!

Well, figuring an investment of $2,850.00 was issued to the attorney already, and patent was still needed (or believed to be needed), a check was issued for $750.00. (Attorney $3,600.00 — Author/me zero).

After completion and changes to my patent were made, the attorney again set a meeting to review the "new" claims. The "new" claims seemed almost the same, except words referring to any electronic apparatus were removed and a general, more specific nature for all claims centered on the actual new product idea. These "new" claims actually detailed my product idea and it's intended uses with a great deal of specifics. A much improved patent, in my opinion. The patent was submitted to the United States Patent and Trademark office for review.

Two months had passed since accepting the additional payment for my "new" patent. Naturally I was uneasy, waiting for an approval statement from the United States Patent and Trademark office. Finally, a letter arrived from my patent attorney. Quickly the feeling of accomplishment and approval overcame me. But wait. The attorney indicated in his letter the United States Patent and Trademark office had rejected three of seven claims submitted. The attorney indicated the United States Patent and Trademark office allows individuals three strikes before you're out. In other words, it was okay the patent review board rejected some of my claims; we still had one chance to address the examiner's concerns and change our claims. Also, the attorney pointed out for him to address the examiner's concerns an additional $750.00 fee was necessary. Well, there was no explanation needed for the feeling which overcame me. This was it! No patent, and I was out $3,600.00.

The attorney explained to me the claims for my patent had overlapped another previous patent, which, it just so happened, was discovered in MY— original patent search. My attorney said the patent examiner had misinterpreted the previous claims cited, and we must dispute their interpretation of claims listed in the patents discovered in our search.

Again, an additional fee was necessary for the attorney's time. This certainly would be the last rendition. The check for $750.00 was issued to the attorney. The patent must be issued; the savings account was empty. (Attorney $4,250.00 — Author/me zero).

Six weeks had passed when finally a letter from my attorney arrived. The letter indicated congratulations were in order. My patent was approved. All right, this is great, finally! But his letter indicated a patent issuance fee was necessary.

This was a standard fee from the United States Patent and Trademark office. The amount of $585.00 was required within three months and an additional $100.00 attorney fee was needed for issuance of my patent. How could another $685.00 be needed when $4,250.00 had already been spent? And why didn't the attorney inform me of all these excessive fees? Oh, well, another check for $685.00 was issued; after all, my patent was approved. The patent was issued at a total cost of **$4,935.00**. Suddenly, the initial fee of $2,250.00 for the original patent seemed rather minuscule. Wouldn't you agree?

As time passed, the investment in my patent began to lose its impact as my savings account began to increase ever so slightly. The patent was received from the United States Patent and Trademark office. Naturally, it was immediately framed and placed above the fireplace mantle. However, it would have looked more appropriate in a safety deposit box. After all, this patent was worth almost $5,000.00. Or was it? Wait . . .

Another letter from my patent attorney had arrived. The letter from my attorney indicated most patents were good or valid for fourteen or seventeen years, depending on the type of patent. (Recall, a Utility Patent is good for seventeen years and a Design Patent is good for fourteen years.) To keep the patent "good," the government charges fees called maintenance/servicing fees. These fees are needed to keep the patent in an "active status." Also, these fees are necessary for clerical duties for all types of patents. The maintenance/service fee was another set of fees never disclosed in the initial patent process.

As of December 1994, the maintenance/service fees were:

Amount Due Years After Date of Patent Issued

3.5 Years	$480.00
7.5 Years	$965.00
11.5 Years	$1,450.00

These fees, again, were never discussed with me by my attorney. Inventor, please beware. These fees can change at anytime, most likely in the upward direction, and you must pay all fees to keep your patent in an active status for the life of the patent!

As you can see, the cost of patenting a new product or idea is extremely expensive. The first fee for patent search, the actual first initial patent writing fee, the patent filing fee, the second edition rewrite fee, the third edition rewrite fee, the patent issue fee, and patent maintenance/service fees. Who knows? The patent could finally cost **$7,830.00** in 1994 dollars after all fees are paid!

Finally, you've discovered most of the fees associated with patenting. Thus, you're more likely to avoid falling victim to the patent SCAM.

The patent scam results from patent attorneys failing to disclose all fees involved with patenting a concept. And, attorneys requesting a small upfront fee suggesting to the inventor this fee is the only money necessary for patenting the new product or idea. As you can see, a patent for an invention is expensive. Don't become a victim and lose thousands and thousands of dollars to this SCAM. Please, take precautions and review this section of the book again! Its for your own protection.

Author's Note

In addition to patent attorneys, a patent agent may construct your patent, if you so choose. Although a patent agent may develop your patent at a reduced cost, when compared to a patent attorney, the agent may not litigate any portion of the patent in a court of law.

OUTLINE OF PATENT PROCESS

A. Concept creation or new product idea.
B. Determine need of new product idea by informal statistics or other means. (See Marketing Section of this book.) If need exists, proceed to "C" of this outline.
C. Development or Concept of a New Invention.
   1. Create Engineering Drawings.
   2. Develop detailed Abstract of Invention.
   3. Create possible prototype (if necessary). Initially proceed without prototype, until a request is made for production units.
D. Patent Process (Choice).
   1. Re-Review Patent & Patent Process Section of this book.
   2. Determine which option you will select. (Patent Attorney, Patent Agent (similar to a Patent Attorney) Write Patent Yourself, "Non-Disclosure" Agreement).
   3. Obtain books from local library or bookstore for supporting your Patent Process choice.
   4. Recall patent search fees from local colleges are cheaper than Patent Attorney fees for said search.
E. Proceed with Marketing Section of this book.

CHAPTER 2

MARKETING AND
THE MARKETING PROCESS

CHAPTER 2

MARKETING AND
THE MARKETING PROCESS

Today many companies and corporations are in business to market many different types of products. These companies and corporations assist individuals by presenting products to industry, thus driving consumers to purchase the products. The idea of presenting a product in a fashion that instinctively drives consumers to feel a need for the product is the marketing process.

The marketing process is the most important part of the invention process to ensure money spent developing the new product idea doesn't go to waste.

As an inventor, witnessing many marketing programs and processes that have developed lack-luster returns, I've assembled some of the most cost effective ways of marketing a new invention on a small fixed budget, mainly the inventors own money. These ideas help maximize market exposure on a relatively small amount of money, and they help inhibit the path of the marketing SCAM. Details on market exposure and the marketing SCAM will follow.

Marketing a product or a new product idea usually involves a process called market research. "Market Research is a five step process, utilizing the scientific method of reasoning.
1. Defining the problem (or need).
2. Analyzing the situation.

34

3. Getting problem specific information (possibly using a market survey for gathering data about your
market).
4. Interpreting data (from the market survey or other
sampling technique).
5. Solving the problem."[2]

Market research helps inventors or manufacturers
determine quantity of potential customers, and it deter-
mines how strong the customer's desire is to purchase the
new product. The research may also determine how and
where consumers demonstrate a need for your product,
and it helps you sell as much of your new product as
possible.

One last point about market research. It will add
value to your new product by allowing you to understand
your consumer's buying habits. Do not overlook this valuable research process. I have included a sample market
survey used in my market research and a brief synopsis
on market surveys later in this book should you decide to
develop your market research by yourself. Additionally,
please consult your local library for more detailed information on developing market research and market surveys. However, if for some reason you cannot perform the
market research yourself, many fine companies are willing to perform the research for a small fee.

Once your market research is completed and your
market research favors investment in your new product
or idea, you must determine how large of an investment or
how small of an investment you will make for developing a
market campaign. It's important to remember marketing a
product is the most important part of a successful invention!
Unfortunately, the amount of money for investment in your
marketing campaign must be determined by remaining monies,
after developing your new invention. Spend appropriately.
(I'll tell you how to spend appropriately later in this book.)

[2]McCarthy, E. Jerome & Perreault, William D. Jr. *Basic Marketing*. Irwin, 1990.

After you've determined the amount of investment for your marketing campaign, you must focus on your consumer and your marketing approach (your product's selling points). Thinking of a consumer, which we all are, I'm sure we've noticed when we have a need for a product, we naturally pay with our hard earned dollars for the product to fulfill our needs. And how we arrive at the conscious decision to purchase the product usually is inspired by an advertisement that demonstrates the product's advantages and how it fulfills our needs.

To develop the advertisement that creates and demonstrates the advantages of your product and the relationship to fulfilling your consumer needs, you must create a marketing campaign. A marketing campaign is an outline type listing of various marketing strategies (selling points of your product) and lists of different advertising sources to display those strategies. In addition, a marketing campaign is a way of controlling variables put together to satisfy a target consumer group.

To develop an award winning marketing campaign, think of the previously mentioned target consumer group. Constrain your marketing campaign to this group's curiosities about your product, while developing the perspective need for your product within your advertisement. Preview the final marketing advertisement selected from your marketing campaign on small test groups to ensure the message you are delivering is clearly understood. You may decide to ask your relatives, friends and significant others to assist you in development and to be the test group for your advertisements. This will help develop a fine marketing campaign tailored to your potential customers or consumers. However, if you've made the unfortunate decision to select a marketing company to create your marketing campaign. PLEASE BE AWARE: You may fall victim to the marketing SCAM. Details on the marketing SCAM follow in a couple of pages.

Author's Note

Most marketing people probably think, and they will tell you they think, marketing a product or developing a marketing campaign is a scientific process. But it's actually not! Marketing a product or developing a marketing campaign is the avenue for you to generate monies from your idea through an induced or implied presented scenario or application of the new product idea to your consumers. The scientific process is the development of the new product or new product idea, and that's the easy part as you will soon note!

Additionally, attempting to scientifically predict how consumers will purchase your product is at best a hypothetical guess that is based on your market research. Please follow my detailed outline to ensure your marketing investments remain at a minimum.

MARKETING PROCESS AND
MARKETING ADVERTISING

Earlier in this section, I told you to "spend appropriately" when it came to marketing your product. Well, you might have asked yourself, "How do I spend appropriately when I don't even know where or how to spend my remaining investment money?" Right? Well, to answer this question, you must begin by defining the types of marketing vehicles or sources most effective for your product or new product idea.

Each year millions of dollars are spent by companies trying to improve and expand their market share, utilizing formal/informal statistics and market research to create an improved marketing campaign. These techniques, as stated, utilize the scientific method to help synthesize market data but fail to blatantly demonstrate where and how companies need to present their products for sale and what types of advertising vehicles are necessary.

Author's Note

Although I will outline for you the various advertising vehicles, it's your decision to choose the most effective advertising vehicle for your product. But don't worry. My detailed methods, listed herein, will ensure you make the right decisions.

When it comes to advertising, without a doubt the most important aspect is gaining the largest viewing and reading audience for the cheapest price. When considering advertising vehicles I've discovered many times that the higher priced network television, national magazines (i.e. *People* magazine, *T.V. Guide, Reader's Digest*), syndicate radio station programs, etc. seemed to provide a greater viewing or reading audience, but they failed to increase my sales. They did, however, quickly deplete my savings acount!

The reason my sales didn't increase is, every new product introduced to market must consider the consumer. How many times have you seen new products on television and failed to be swayed by the advertisement? Did you run right out and purchase the product? Probably not. Well, the same is true for small inventor's products.

Unfortunately, many small inventors cannot afford to run the advertisements over and over (this is advertising frequency which is detailed later in this section) as large companies do, until a potential consumer begins to associate a "need" with the product.

However, utilizing my marketing approach, many advertising options remain for small inventors to increase frequency of their product(s) without depleting their savings account. Let's investigate some of my advertising options.

One of my favorite marketing vehicles/advertisements, probably the most successful in terms of Return on Investment (ROI), is a Product Press Release. A Product Press Release usually describes in detail, similar to an abstract, the wonderful advantages of owning or having your new product. Press Releases are made of eye catching color schemes, such as fuchsia, contain the name of your company, your telephone number (preferably a 1-800-xxx-xxxx, which can be set-up on your home phone), address, intended customer or consumer, cost, reasons for / "need", intended marketing plan or distribution network, and photo of your product, all detailed within a single page. Also, any other information used to inform the consumer of your product is explained within the single page Press Release. A sample of a Product Press Release is presented on the next page for your review.

Further, the Press Release is the most cost effective way I know for obtaining large viewership and readership for your product with only the cost of printing and distributing within your market. Also, be sure to include your consumers directly or indirectly through the following public information sources.

Today may newspapers, television stations, radio stations and magazines contain a new product section for information retrieved from various Press Releases. Almost every newspaper, television station, radio station and magazine nationwide receives hundreds of Press Releases each day announcing new products. Thus, for your Press Release to be displayed in the sources mentioned above, your Press Release must be a standout and must contain all details listed herein, so that any information source receiving your Press Release can announce the details without having to call for additional information about your product.

To obtain a list of newspapers, television stations, radio stations and magazines for distribution of your Press Release, most libraries or list companies provide a detailed source of information on the various distribution sources herein. This information contains the names of individuals

 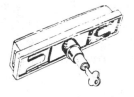

**PRESS
INFORMATION**

<u>Vide-O-Lock</u> for games like Nintendo ®

<u>For Immediate Release</u>   <u>Contact Martin Smith</u>
(800) 444-6783
(602) 582-3878

VIDEO GAMES VS. HOMEWORK, AND THE WINNER IS . . . ?

Is your child a video junkie? Would he rather nail a video spaced alien than an A in math? Does he spend more time with the Mario Brothers than his own? Video games provide hours of entertainment for young minds, but in an era when both parents often work, it can be difficult to monitor playtime. Difficult, that is, until now! **MPT Electronics*** of Phoenix, Arizona has found a way to ensure that the games don't begin until the homework and chores are finished.

The **Vide-O-Lock** for games like Nintendo® is made of durable **ABS Plastic** and locks securely into any (NES) Nintendo® game slot rendering it inaccessible to youngsters. The device utilizes a specially designed **National Lock** made of brass and comes equipped with two keys allowing parents to use their own discretion when it comes to play time.

Video games can be both fun and challenging for kids. But now, the Vide-O-Lock puts parents in charge of the joystick, so the work is done before the fun begins.

The suggested retail price of the **Vide-O-Lock** is $9.95 and is being marketed nationally by MPT Electronics.

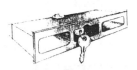

Vide-O-Lock for VCRs
Also available from MPT, the Video Securing Device. The VSD locks securely into any front loading video cassette recorder protecting the sensitive electronics from the curiosity of small children.

*MPT Electronics is not associated with Nintendo America

■ MPT ELECTRONICS ■ 18624 N. 15TH PLACE ■ PHOENIX, AZ 85024 ■
(800) 444-MPTE ■ (602) 582-3878 ■

or New Product Editors, their phone numbers, and addresses where you should send your Press Release. By sending your Press Release to these sources and for only the price of a stamp and printing, you can gain local and national exposure for your new product. What are you waiting for? (Get your Press Release in the mail.)

Author's Note

In addition to announcing your new product to the above mentioned information sources, a Product Press Release can also serve as your commuinication to distributors and market representatives to begin or increase wholesale purchasing activity.

As you can see, a Product Press Release is an important beginning for any new product idea. And many inventors feel with limited advertising budgets the Press Release is the only advertising vehicle they need. However, after being asked many times by new inventors, "Is the Press Release the only information or advertising vehicle I need?" I still respond, "Maybe or maybe not." It all depends on the successfulness of your Press Release to create sales. However, if you feel additional marketing tools may be necessary, because your sales weren't as good as expected from using only your Press Release, the next most cost effective marketing tool may be a Market Product Brochure.

MARKET PRODUCT BROCHURE

A Market Product Brochure, an excellent additional market information source, lists complete details about your new product. These Product Brochures are similar to Press Releases.Yet, they contain more details about the new product and the company selling the product. They, The Product Brochures, usually are distributed in various places, such as product display seminars, in front of your local grocery store or to corporate buyers, and they may help generate additional sales above a Press Release, if the brochure looks really good.

Although most companies use a two-fold, multi-colored brochure with bright graphics filled with specific information on the new product, you may, depending on your marketing budget, choose to create your brochure to your specifications. But please remember the old saying to ensure that you're not wasting valuable advertising dollars. "The eye appealing brochure will present better than the plain Jane brochure!" So, use some common sense when developing your brochure. Create the most impressive brochure of its kind and avoid wasting your hard earned money. This may be your only contact with some of your customers.

Additionally, if your funding doesn't support the Product Brochure, as my budget didn't, you may replace the brochure with the really nice Press Release you designed previously. It's your choice. On to larger advertising sources or vehicles.

MARKET ADVERTISING AND
THE MARKETING SCAM

Since more and more people today have cable television, let's talk about placing advertising there. Today, cable television is becoming the advertising vehicle of most new inventors and many large companies select it over the big three networks, ABC, CBS and NBC, for reasons such as reduced cost, better availability and increased frequency. Although many large companies can afford the costs to run commercials on the big three networks (ABC, NBC, CBS), many still decide, as do small inventors, to advertise on cable television for increased potential frequency and the reduced cost.

You will recall earlier in this section that I mentioned advertising frequency as the number of times a potential customer may be exposed to your advertisement and that the cost to advertise was/is extremely important! I don't mean to repeat myself, but this is very, very important!

The more often a potential customer sees your advertisement the greater the chance becomes the customer will associate the new product and the "need" being demonstrated in your advertisement. And if the cost of advertising is the cheapest available, you are able to advertise the commercial a greater number of times with the same amount of money. Thus, the more times you air your commercial, increasing the advertising frequency, the greater your chances become that your new consumers will recall or remember your product. And that's the only reason any company or corporation advertises. This is why frequency and cost of advertising is so important.

As you can see, frequency is very important, and cable television can provide a greater frequency over the big three networks, because, guess why, that's right, the cost to advertise is about half the price of the big three networks' cost.

Here's my example of advertising on cable television, some pitfalls of advertising and, we must not forget, the **MARKETING SCAM.**

To advertise my Vide-O-Lock[3] for Nintendo[4] Games, my marketing campaign determined advertising straight to potential customers, no wholesale options (vertical marketing only), because my costs to produce the Vide-O-Lock were too high. I decided to develop a 30-second commercial to advertise my product based upon my market research which indicated a majority of my potential customers, which were adults, could be reached with a minimal per customer cost through cable television stations. A toll free phone number was set-up to handle calls (1-800-444-6783 if you would like a Vide-O-Lock) and to be featured in the 30-second commercial.

Further, my marketing campaign determined a 30-

[3]Vide-O-Lock is registered trademark of MPT Electronics, Inc.
[4]Nintendo is a registered trademark of Nintendo of America, Inc.

second commercial over a 60-second commercial, because the cost to air the commercial was half of what a 60-second commercial cost on cable television. Thus, the 30-second commercial increased advertising frequency with the same amount of advertising dollars, a huge benefit.

Remember, with new product to market introductions, again, frequency is very important! And when airing a commercial on television *reach* is also important. *Reach* is just the number of people who might be watching the program when your commercial airs. I'll explain advertising pitfalls concerning *reach* shortly.

To produce the 30-second commercial, three separate production companies were asked to bid. These companies quoted prices for the production from $4,500.00 to $7,000.00. That was a lot of money for only 30-seconds of film! Obviously, the price was out of my range. Now what?

You may, as I did, begin thinking of the many friends and acquaintances who might be able to help produce the commercial. Yes! It just so happened a friend of mine, how lucky, was in the production film business. He produced my commercial for half of the lowest bid at around $2,000.00.

Author's Note

If you don't have access to a "friend" or an acquaintance to help produce your commercial, the best bet is to look for a new production company. These companies usually are more willing to negotiate a better price for production to help establish their businesses. To find a "newer" production company, contact your Better Business Bureau. Also, never disclose the amount of money you plan to spend with the production company, until you have a final decision on the type of production for your advertising. Your advertising budget may be small, as was mine, and many companies do not provide the attention you deserve, if they realize the size of your advertising budget.

The next step, after producing my commercial, was to review the 30-second production for clear demonstrated uses of the Vide-O-Lock for Nintendo[5] Games. Although I wanted to introduce both of my products in one production (the Video Securing Device for VCRs and the Vide-O-Lock for Nintendo[6] games), the 30-second commercial focused on the one particular product, the Vide-O-Lock for Nintendo[7] Games.

The 30-second commercial was presented to a focus group (as I suggested earlier), and it appeared excellent. The advantages to owning a Vide-O-Lock were clear, according to my test participants. The selling points presented were non-aggressive, not to offend customers, but the need for my product was solid and displayed as such. Now, it was time to define my market segment (select my demographics) for advertising.

To determine or develop the right market segment, you must spend a lot of time researching potential consumers, as I did. You must identify the demographics of your market (age, gender, income, number of children, single or married, etc.) and prepare a market research tool to gather more informnation about your market. You must review the results of your research, and in my case, based on ninety-five percent confidence level in our market survey; one in four families owning a Nintendo[8] Game with children under the age of thirteen had a need for our Vide-O-Lock.

Author's Note

It may appear we performed the market research after developing the product, but we actually performed the market research prior to investing in the patent,

---

[5]Nintendo is a registered trademark of Nintendo of America, Inc.
[6]Nintendo registered trademark of Nintendo of America, Inc.
[7]Nintendo trademark of Nintendo of America, Inc.
[8]Nintendo registered trademark of Nintendo of America, Inc.

production molds and materials required to make the Vide-O-Lock. A copy of our market survey is included on page 47 for your review.

———————

After receiving my market research data, which was to help me understand my market segment, I realized I only understood somewhat — how to advertise my product. The market research couldn't tell me what television shows, what time slots, or even what television stations would generate the best sales for my product. I felt stuck between a rock and a hard place. I needed some so called "expert" advice. I guessed it meant seeking the assistance of a good marketing company. A big mistake, as you will soon read.

The first market company consulted called, — well, I can't say, it's on the West Coast — sold a lot of air time for cable television across the country. A conversation began between a market representative from the company and myself.

The representative asked, "Will 60-seconds of air time per commercial be needed — or greater?

My response, "No, only a 30-second block of air time is needed."

"Okay, what kind of product is it?" he asked.

I replied, "A Vide-O-Lock for Nintendo[9] Games."

"What?"

"It's a Vide-O-Lock for Nintendo[10] Games; it's a new product. I invented it myself."

"How much can you afford to spend?" Naturally, a representative's favorite question.

I replied, "Well, under $3,000.00."

"Okay, I'll see what I can come up with. Call you in a few days with prices on air time for cable television."

[9]Nintendo registered trademark of Nintendo of America, Inc.
[10]Nintendo registered trademark of Nintendo of America, Inc.

A couple of days passed. And a thought occurred to me. The advertising company didn't even ask me about my market segment (demographics). It couldn't be they were performing the market research to tailor my product to a specific market, could it?

Think again. The representative called me back three days later. He suggested I try to spend a little more money; this way, he could get a much better deal on 30-second air time per unit block. The larger the blocks of commercial air time purchased at the same time, the better the per unit price. But I was limited to the $3,000.00 and didn't appreciate the representative's nonchalant attitude towards my hard-earned money. If only I hadn't informed the representative on the amount of money I had planned to spend, then I would have received more respect from the representative.

The discussion continued on commercial time and how to display the 30-second piece. I informed the representative that he had failed to ask my demographics. Immediately, he insisted we were just in the beginning stages of negotiations and didn't require demographics! However, he now asked for the demographics which seemed sort of confusing to me.

We discussed the Vide-O-Lock's advantages and who the commercial was selling. We discovered many interesting markets. We chose a market segment with an average of 2.3 children per household, and the children were within age ranges my market survey recommended (13 years and younger). A higher than median per annual household income, and an adult age range from 25-to-39 years old. Also, I requested a high saturation of cable television (large reach potential). The market representative agreed with all my demographic selections, and the selections were all based upon my market research data. Thus, the market representative, just as I thought didn't perform any market research at all.

The representative went to work on my market. A few days passed (maybe a week), and I finally received a call. The representative informed me there were multiple

MARKET SURVEY
VIDE-O-LOCK FOR NINTENDO GAMES

1. DO YOU OWN A NINTENDO GAME?
   _____ YES _____ NO.
2. DO YOU HAVE A NEED TO RESTRICT THE USE OF NINTENDO IN YOUR HOUSEHOLD?
   _____ YES _____ NO
3. DO YOU HAVE CHILDREN? _____YES _____ NO.
   IF YES, HOW MANY ___?
4. BASED ON YOUR ANSWER TO QUESTION #3, LIST YOUR CHILDREN(S) BIRTH DATE(S).
5. HAS NINTENDO IN YOUR HOUSEHOLD INTERFERED WITH THE HOMEWORK, CHORES OR OTHER ACTIVITIES OF YOUR CHILDREN? _____ YES _____NO
6. HOUSEHOLD INCOME RANGE IN DOLLARS
   (check best range.)
   0-$20,000 ___ $20,001.00 - $40,000.00 ___
   $40,001.00 - $60,000.00 ____ $60,001.00 - up ____
7. HOW OFTEN DO YOUR CHILDREN OR YOURSELF USE THE NINTENDO GAME?
   Daily____ Once a Week ____ Twice a Week _
   Three Times a Week ____ Four Times a Week ____
   Five Times a Week ____ Six Times a Week ____
   Once a Month ____ Other ___
8. LIST YOUR ZIP CODE BELOW.
   My zip code is:_____
9. THE VIDE-O-LOCK FOR NINTENDO GAMES ALLOWS PARENTS TO DECIDE WHEN IT'S NINTENDO TIME, THUS ALLOWING "HOMEWORK" AND "CHORES" TO COME FIRST. IN YOUR OPINION, WHAT PRICE RANGE DO YOU FEEL THE DEVICE SHOULD SELL FOR?
   (check best answer, values in dollars.)
   00.00 - $5.00 ____ $5.01 - $10.00 ____
   $10.01 - $15.00 ____ $15.01 - $20.00 ____
10. BASED ON YOUR ANSWER TO QUESTION NUMBER NINE, INDICATE YOUR WILLINGNESS TO PURCHASE THE "VIDE-O-LOCK" FOR NINTENDO GAMES AT THE PRICE YOU SUGGESTED (circle best answer).
    UNCERTAIN   1   2   3   4   5   6   7   CERTAIN

areas with similar demographics which I had recommended. He FAXed me a copy of recommended cable television stations and recommended regions in which to air my commercial. The representative suggested places like San Diego and Los Angeles, California, Syracuse, New York, a few places in Illinois, Phoenix, Arizona, Rochester, New York, and Dallas, Texas. The representative also suggested cable television stations within these areas like MTV, USA Network, Lifetime, ESPN, TNT, WGN and Fox. These stations all differed in price and possible *reach* (populations varied). He, then, recommended all the cable television stations based on their availability and price per 30-second spot. It was now my decision to choose the station and location to air my commercial.

Author's Note

Although the market representative did not try to hustle me on possible households within each market, you must not forget that the number of possible households usually specified for a population in a selected area is Total Households, not the actual cable subscribing households. Don't be fooled by this Marketing SCAM.

My decision, based on my data, was to air my commercials in San Diego and Los Angeles, California with cable stations USA, TNT, and Lifetime, and in Rochester, New York, with cable stations USA, TNT and MTV. In addition, I chose a small segment on MTV and Lifetime in Phoenix, Arizona, so I could see my own commercials.

The reasons I chose these areas: the most possible frequency for the lowest price, comparatively speaking. The total price to run fifty spots in San Diego on a rotor (anytime — 6:00 a.m. through 12:00 midnight for each day selected) was $1,260.00 in 1993 dollars. The prices for the other areas were higher, but the average 30-second commercial was $25.00 per spot in the areas specified above. A lot of money for a little time!

Although the price for the commercials was high, I knew the representative must have received some sort of commission for his efforts, even though he really did very little work. I figured the commission was small, so I really didn't worry about it.

A few more weeks went by, and my sales from the commercials were okay. However, instead of being happy about receiving some sales, I was thinking my sales were not good enough, and had I not paid any commission to the advertising representative, I could have run more commercials, resulting in more sales. Another empty feeling from the loss of more money.

A couple more days passed when suddenly I received a call from a company in Las Vegas, Nevada; the company wanted to discuss my commercials. (I can't say the name of the company.) They offered me some thirty commercial spots in the same regions I had just advertised in for a hell of a lot less money than what I had just paid. They offered the same number of rotor cable television spots, 30-seconds in length, in Rochester, New York, on stations MTV, USA Network, TNT, and ESPN for $300.00. Further, they offered me one hundred 30-second commercials for that $300.00. I couldn't believe it! I had paid *four* times that amount for the same spots (same location and cable television stations). I felt ill. Again, I couldn't believe how many times through this invention process and marketing process I had fallen victim to the Patent and Marketing SCAM. This was pathetic that I'd lost so much *money* to all these con-artists!

After a painful two weeks, I finally regained my self-esteem. I'd realized this Patent and Marketing SCAM affected every new product inventor, and I was not the only inventor to have excessively paid for every little bit of assistance. I felt as if every marketing company or patent attorney was a joke. However, I received another call from the Las Vegas marketing company which informed me of the Marketing SCAM. They further informed me representatives for various cable televisions sell air time for as much money as they can possibly get! Obviously, I was now well aware of this! Also, the Las

Vegas company told me cable television stations would sell air time directly to any advertiser. This meant I was able to buy my own air time and save additional advertising agency fees.

After the conversation with the communications company, I called the representative in Los Angeles, California. He informed me the fees I paid were "normal" air time prices, and the advertising fee of twenty-five percent was a standard commission fee absorbed by the advertising agency he represented. This meant, naturally, I could have saved myself hundreds and hundreds of dollars by just calling the cable companies where I decided to run my commercials directly. After all, the representative in California did nothing but make a few phone calls, and he received twenty-five percent of my hard earned dollars!

The advertising fee or agency fee discussed herein usually averages fifteen to twenty-five percent of the total advertising bill. These fees are either paid directly to an advertising agency from the advertiser or the fees may be added directly to the cost of advertising and passed on to the client. Although I questioned the market representative on why the cost of advertising was so high, I want you to know, he still failed to disclose the additional twenty-five percent advertising fee which I had paid until I asked the questions directly. This was the Marketing SCAM.

ADDITIONAL PRESS RELEASE
INFORMATION

If someone asked me today, as many inventors have, "Where or how should I gain the most market exposure for my product with such little money to advertise?" I would suggest the product Press Release. As I mentioned, the product Press Release is a cost effective tool which allows inventors the possibility of national exposure for only the cost of printing and mailing.

While creating your Press Release, be sure to include all information detailed earlier and arrange the information in an appealing fashion. Also, ensure your distribution includes any publication dealing with your type of product, such as specialized magazines, newsletters, television stations, newspapers or otherwise.

Although I may have not enlightened you as an inventor on all the possible marketing vehicles, such as expensive infomercials, a thirty-minute commercial type production, marketing coupons, advertisement clips usually generated to allow consumers a specified price reduction to inspire new product sales, and co-op advertising, fees usually paid by the manufacturer for advertising their products and the retailer's name that will sell your products, I did, however, offer the advertising vehicles which have generated the greatest benefit for inventors on small fixed budgets. These vehicles allow inventors the largest viewing or reading audience for the cheapest price.

If you would like more information on infomercials, market coupons or co-op advertising, your local library contains a great deal of specific information relating to these topics.

SUMMARY OF THE MARKETING PROCESS AND LESSONS LEARNED

Today, marketing a new product is extremely tricky. In fact, many inventors have excellent products but fail to gain financial freedom because their marketing programs are ineffective.

An ineffective marketing program, as you will recall, usually results from the failure of inventors to perform in-depth market research, prior to investment. Without market research, regarding an inventor's target market, a lack of knowledge and understanding is the result.

However, if an inventor performs the market research, the benefits will be tremendous. The data will determine the consumer's needs and will allow the inventor to create the right marketing program, focused on the consumer's needs.

Although creating the right marketing program may be a hit and miss type process, you must remember to continue learning about your consumers, using market surveys, and be willing to constantly change your marketing program for the ever changing consumer's needs. This may be expensive, but you will minimize your advertising costs by using your Press Release as many times as possible, until your revenue allows you to develop either a magazine, newspaper or television commercial type advertisement.

Once you've developed your advertisement, research your market selections and demographics, using information provided either by your local library or advertising source (magazine, newspaper, or television station where you plan to display your advertisement). Place your advertisement, being fully aware of the fifteen to twenty-five percent advertising agency fee which you will save by placing the advertisement directly yourself. Then, be prepared to receive orders.

Author's Note

It's been said the greatest products in the world will sell themselves. However, a lot of inventors will disagree! No matter if your invention is simple, complex or considered to be the greatest in the world, a good marketing plan is essential to help sell your product. Inventor, please don't get discouraged, if your sales don't reach record levels right away. Mine didn't. Try again with a new marketing plan and continue developing these new marketing plans, until your sales do reach the levels you've always wanted. I didn't give up. So, inventor, please don't. Rewards will come.

If there's one important thing I would like every inventor to remember about the marketing of a new product idea, is not to let yourself get discouraged by your initial sales. Most inventors get easily discouraged by less than favorable initial sales. This causes countless possibilities to slip through their hands, as well the possibility of becoming this great nation's next millionaire. Also, avoid the Marketing SCAM by the process described herein to eliminate the discouraging effect of losing thousands and thousands of dollars. Stay positive, and continue to search for the pot of gold at the end of your rainbow. Someday, with persistence, it will happen. Keep trying!

Let's now look into ways to avoid the last and ultimate SCAM, the invention companies SCAM.

MARKETING PROCESS OUTLINE

A. Market Survey
  1. Develop Market Survey:
     a. Develop survey questions focused on the consumers need of product, willingness to purchase, price consumers are willing to pay and demographics (age, sex, number of children, household income ranges, etc.).
     b. Reference example Market Survey this chapter for additional questions.
  2. Develop Statistical Application:
     a. Market survey questions must use a statistical application scale such as a Likeret scale.
       Strongly Agree   Strongly Disagree
         1   2   3   4   5
       or "YES" or "NO" probability scale.
     b. Reference example Market Survey this chapter for additional questions.
  3. Determine Number of participants based upon your level of confidence within your survey.
  4. Distribute and Collect surveys.
  5. Synthesize Data using T-Distribution, Z-Distribution. Analysis of Variance (ANOVA) or CHI square statis-

tical applications.
6. Learn from your results.
B. Advertising Your Product and Development of Your Marketing Campaign.
   1. Detertine the amount of money you may spend for advertising of your product.
   2. Develop and Distribute product Press Release to various sources as defined within this section.
      a. Setup an 1-800-xxx-xxxx number on your home phone.
      b. Develop your company name and business. Ascertain State, Local, and Federal approved licenses.
      c. Set up Bank Account. (You may choose to do this later, depending on sales.)
   3. Develop Product Brochure as detailed within this section. (This may or may not be applicable, depending on your advertising budget.)
   4. Develop Cable Television station advertisement. (Again, depending on your advertising budget.)
      a. Place advertisements, using your demographics from your market research. Place advertisement directly with a cable company, avoiding advertising agency fee.
   5. Re-Develop / Re-Think your marketing campaign and advertisements, learning from your past experiences.
C. Develop Wholesale, Distributor Businesses, and Market Representatives.
   1. Send inquiries to market representatives and distributors.
   2. Contact large retailers. Send inquiries related to purchasing your product for wholesale price.
   3. Distribute your Product Press Release and Product Brochure to wholesalers, distributors and market representatives.
   4. Continue researching new marketing and new sales opportunities.

CHAPTER 3

INVENTION COMPANIES AND THE INVENTION COMPANY PROCESS

CHAPTER 3

INVENTION COMPANIES AND THE INVENTION COMPANY PROCESS

How many times, while watching the late night show or while watching television in general, have you seen a commercial asking, "Do you have a new invention or new product idea, and if so, you need to call XYZ Invention Company immediately." Have you seen these commercials a couple of times, a few times or more?

Well, fact is, you've probably seen these commercials many times, but you paid little attention, until the time you conceived your new product idea and decided you'd like to become a millionaire from your idea. However, your dreams of becoming a millionaire may have dissolved the second you decided to call XYZ Invention Company. The reasons are simple and will be detailed throughout this section on Invention Companies and their SCAMS. Also it is important to know that many new inventors never learn these secrets, until after they've lost thousands and thousands of their hard earned dollars to XYZ Invention Company or similar invention companies for very little meaningful assistance. However, by reading this book and understanding my methods, you will avoid this blatant deception.

If you think about it logically, invention companies, like XYZ or any other invention company, are not in business to make millionaires or successful inventors, but simply are in business to make thousands and thousands of dollars from each inventor for developing ineffective product Press Releases, marketing brochures, and fancy pictures of what the new product "MAY" eventually look like. These invention companies usually provide very little statistical market research or engineering prints for development of your new product, both of which are an essential part of marketing and developing your new idea.

Further, these invention companies usually provide very little effective material for assisting new inventors, and unfortunately I've seen many examples of new inventors falling victim to these invention companies and their SCAMS. However, by reading this section and following my guidelines, you'll receive invaluable information on how to avoid invention companies. Plus, you'll understand the fatal mistakes many inventors make, hoping to introduce their new inventions or products to market utilizing the teachings of many invention assistance companies.

As you read this chapter, you may note the many injustices performed by such companies like XYZ Invention Company and their like, and you'll probably feel sorry for some inventors who solicit invention companies for assistance. However, you will avoid invention companies and their SCAMS, because, as a successful inventor, I will reveal these injustices and inform you of situations and questions needed to avoid the SCAM associated with some invention companies should you choose this option for introducing your new idea to market.

Here's a detailed example of an invention company SCAM. The product is imaginary, but the example is real.

Let's say, for example, I've conceived an idea or new product that I want to introduce and market. Naturally, I feel my new product will revolutionize its market, the hose and sock industry, and I've decided to call my product the "Adjustable Tube Sock".

Knowing that my product is an excellent product and an opportunity to become rich, I decide I'd better market and develop my product immediately. So, I begin looking for ideas or assistance to bring my product to market.

Thinking of the many advantages for any consumer

who purchases my sock, I note my product, the "Adjust-able Tube Sock" will avoid the annoying problem of sock material building up at the bottom of shoes, resulting from the sock sliding down the wearer's leg, once the material has stretched-out. Feeling as if my product prevents this problem by allowing for adjustment when it becomes apparent that the material has stretched out. I realize the uncomfortable feeling of sock material building up at the bottom of a consumer's shoes is avoided. Also, I note, many consumers have different types and sizes of legs, thus the "Adjustable Tube Sock" can be adjusted to fit any size leg. Hence, my sock will work for all consumers who purchase my extremely beneficial product.

I feel my product is worthy, and I begin looking for investors, since I haven't the extra money to invest myself. But nobody is interested, so I begin thinking of other ways to acquire money for investment in my new product. Maybe putting a second mortgage on my house would help, but quickly I decide not to jeopardize my family's well being on my socks, or anything else for that matter. I decide to ask my parents and family about their feelings towards my idea and the possibility of making a small investment in my product. However, I still fail to locate the money needed to introduce my "Adjustable Tube Sock" to market. Then, one night, while watching an old Dracula movie, it happens. A commercial appears, asking individuals if they have great ideas, and if so, they need to call XYZ Invention Company immediately. Quickly, I jump out of bed, turn on the light, and grab the first thing I can find to write down the toll free 800 telephone number.

The next morning, having very little sleep from all my excitement, I call XYZ Invention Company. An operator answers, asking me my name, phone number and address. She informs me XYZ Invention Company will send me — at no obligation — some information pertaining to my idea. She says, "You should receive the information in about four-to-six weeks.

Wait! "Can't I speak to someone about my idea now!"

"No, I'm sorry. I'm just the operator. You'll have to

wait for the information."

Three weeks pass, and finally my information from XYZ Invention Company arrives. Quickly, I open the envelope and find ten pages or so of information, explaining the history of XYZ Invention Company, the services provided by XYZ and some literature, explaining how to submit my idea to XYZ for consideration. Also, included in the information package, are some really nice pictures and Press Releases on successful products introduced to market by XYZ Invention Company and royalties paid by companies who now manufacture some inventor's product.

Following the instructions in the information package, I spend a few days writing a paragraph about my product. The paragraph informs XYZ Invention Company what my product is and how I feel it should be marketed. Also, XYZ requests I sign a "Non-Disclosure" form, which is included in the package, and include a sketch of my product.

After returning the information, a few weeks go by, and finally I received a call from XYZ Invention Company. They want to discuss some options for my product, and we arrange a meeting. Wow! I can't believe it. Immediately, I tell my wife, inform my family, and begin dreaming of the new house I'd always wanted. Heck, I thought I'd even take all of my family to Disney Land.

We'd set a meeting to discuss my "Adjustable Tube Socks." I was surprised to learn XYZ Invention Company had a local office in Phoenix, Arizona, near my home, but no problem. I am ready to sell my idea to anyone for thousands and thousands of dollars. Who cares if they have a local office or are located in Nebraska? I'm ready to sell!

Finally, the day arrives to sit down with the representatives of XYZ Invention Company. I decide I better wear a tie and look really sharp. After all, this might be the only way out of my current job, so what's a few hours more of neck pain.

The XYZ gentleman introduces himself. He says, "I understand you have a product which will revolutionize the hose and sock industry."

Wow, that's my words! "Yes, I sure do!"

He asks me to show him my ideas about my "Adjustable Tube Sock," how it worked, who the consumers are and where or whom might purchase my idea.

I give him the works! I know he's sold. I'm finished.

Well, that's an excellent idea and here's what XYZ Invention Company can do for you. We can prepare a brief synopsis about your product, develop and help introduce to MANUFACTURERS (remember manufacturers are not consumers) your idea through some really great lay-outs and marketing information. We can develop your product portfolio and provide the necessary assistance any inventor needs to introduce their (your) product to market." The XYZ representative then hands me a booklet full of other products successfully introduced to manufacturers by XYZ Invention Company and some photos of recent inventors who were now receiving commissions and royalties, all because of XYZ Invention Company. "What do you think of that."

I'm impressed. XYZ will provide all these things, but at what cost? Just a small commission of payment from my product once it's sold? Ha, here comes the tricky part.

The XYZ Invention Company representative asks me what I feel all the services, explaining each service again, would be worth, considering I am on my way to becoming rich from my "Adjustable Tube Sock."

I think about it for a moment, then respond, "It depends on how much work or time XYZ Invention Company has spent on my product and how much money I'm going to make from the success of my product."

The representative then pulls out the "Standard Fees." Without itemizing the price for each service, the cost is around $3,500.00.

My stomach and my mouth both drop. I ask why the costs are so high and inform the representative the price is well out of my range.

He agrees to reduce the price to ONLY $3,000.00 and offers some financing. He explains the cost would only be around $100.00 a month for all the excellent services provided by XYZ Invention Company and requests I sign the forms already prepared.

How did the representative know I would signup? Confusing, but I ask to borrow his pen.

After agreeing to the financing, XYZ Invention Company starts to work on my project. Informed by the representative only a few weeks are necessary for all the information described above, I eagerly await my XYZ Invention Company package. Finally, XYZ completes my project, excluding market research or engineering prints. XYZ Invention Company provides, as agreed, a beautifully written Press Release, a few copies of a Market Product Brochure and some great sketches of what my product may actually look like.

Wondering how they knew what my product looked like, I scornfully review all the provided information. The sketches seem rather incomplete, though the details of all information provided seem pretty good. However, I do notice a few problems with some information and ask for some improvements.

After completing my review of XYZ Invention Company's project and accepting the final outcome, another chapter in the XYZ Saga opens. For my package to be distributed to "Manufacturers," (not consumers or retailers), I need to provide mailing and other expenses.

"But wasn't all of my expenses covered in my original $3,000.00?"

The representative informs me, "No, distribution of roughly 1,000 packages and mailing fees are necessary to cover postage, handling and the materials."

I can't believe it.

I ask for the manufacturer's distribution list, so I may send my package to the manufactures myself. But XYZ Invention Company refuses.

I insist they provide me all copies of my $3,000.00 invention package and provide me a distribution list for my product.

XYZ Invention Company instead provides me all originals for my package and refuses to give me the distribution list.

Yes, this is an invention company SCAM.

Here is the end of my money and my options with the XYZ Invention Company, and this was the end of my wonderful invention. Broke, desperate and out of money I begin to think the Invention Company SCAM must affect many, many new inventors. And, sure enough, almost every new inventor at one time or another is contacted and affected by the Patent, Market and Invention Company SCAM.

The Invention Company SCAM, described above, is real, and I've seen first-hand many new inventors falling victim to this terrible deception. However, as an inventor myself, I now know how to avoid this dreadful deception, and now so do you.

Please be careful in all your dealings with so called Invention Assistant Companies and avoid the loss of your hard earned dollars by avoiding any such SCAMS as described in this book.

Having acted many times as a free consultant to all inventors, who have requested assistance or who have purchased or read my book, I've seen many examples of similar invention companies and their SCAMS, and the sorrowful effect they have on their victims. In addition, many victims of these SCAMS paid all requested fees, including all mailing, distribution and development expenses, yet received little or no royalties or payments for their new product ideas. In fact, most victims received nothing but a huge loss of money, a feeling of vulnerability and an empty feeling for being manipulated.

My only hope for future inventors is that every inventor possesses a copy of my book. We (inventors) must protect ourselves at all costs and avoid all SCAMS associated with our new product ideas. Please feel free to call me at 1-800-444-6783 with direct and specific questions, regarding the Patent, Marketing and Invention Company SCAM.

CLOSING COMMENTS

In closing, if I could reach out and speak to each and every new inventor, prior to their investment in any new product idea, certainly I would be able to save each and every one of them thousands and thousands of their hard earned dollars. However, realizing that idea is impossible, I decided to detail all my dealings and findings, relating to the Patent, Marketing and Invention Company SCAM, in this book.

I realize many people often dream of becoming millionaires from their new inventions, and that's okay. But beginning any new process or program in the vast game of life, we all require some sort of training.

Every day in your chosen career path, we are all learning and creating new and improved ideas for making our jobs easier. Whether we are being formally trained to learn a new skill or job technique, or teaching a family member a new trade, we all require some sort of educational background to ensure the proper results. The same is true for all inventors and the processes inventors use to achieve their ultimate goal, financial freedom.

This book was designed to help every new product introduced to market by an inventor with only his/her own financial resources.

I can't guarantee using all of my methods will provide the ultimate financial freedom which you desire from your new product. However, I can guarantee by using my methods detailed within this short and easy how-to book you will avoid the Patent, Marketing and Invention Company SCAM.

Again, I lost thousands and thousands of my hard-earned dollars to the Patent, Marketing and Invention Company SCAM. And I personally can't stand so-called honest and ethical businesses preparing the world's greatest entrepreneurs for ultimate deception.

This ultimate deception inspired this and several other books prepared by a lonely inventor in a hostile and corrupt profit-yielding world. I hope I will help you save thousands and thousands of dollars. Congratulations on your new product idea. This and every country was founded on the ingenuity of every human being with great new product ideas similar to your ideas. Happy inventing. Keep up the **GOOD** work!

CONFIDENTIAL
DISCLOSURE AGREEMENT

Subject Matter:

Place of Disclosure:

In consideration of a disclosure of Confidential Information relating to the above-identified subject matter to be made by _____ to the undersigned who desires to receive such information for evaluation or other purposes, such Confidential Information including, but not limited to, all information relating to all inventions and improvements embodied therein and any and all information relating thereto either previously or hereinafter disclosed either orally or in writing, the undersigned hereby agrees that such disclosure shall be treated as CONFIDENTIAL and that the disclosed information pertaining to improved methods and/or apparatus concerning the above-identified subject matter shall not be used in any manner by the undersigned or duplicated or disclosed to others without first obtaining written permission from _____ .

Signature

Firm Name

Date

(This page may be photocopied.)

ABOUT THE AUTHOR
MARTIN C. SMITH
INVENTOR & CONSULTANT

Martin Christopher Smith, an experienced inventor with several different new product ideas and patents, has successfully introduced to market the Vide-O-Lock for games like Nintendo in 1992 and the Video Securing Device for front loading Video Cassette Recorders (VCR) in 1990. Smith has also contributed to several different new product ideas through a "free" information consultant role for new product idea inventors.

After introduction of the Vide-O-Lock and Video Securing Device, Smith began to consult with several new product inventors. After reviewing well over 200 different new product ideas, Smith realized a pattern had developed.

All new product idea inventors had fallen victim to a serious and highly deceptive business practice, preying on the inventor's feelings and emotions, called the Patent, Marketing and Invention Company SCAM.

Smith, realizing he himself had fallen victim to this atrocious deception, decided to document and outline a step-by-step process for all new inventors to avoid Patent, Marketing and Invention Company SCAMS. Additionally, Smith developed a process for all new inventors to introduce their new product ideas to market on a small fixed budget (namely the inventor's own money).

Today, with the knowledge of Smith's book. *How to*

Avoid Patent, Marketing and Invention Company SCAMSs, sub-titled, Wow, *What a Great Idea . . . Now What?,* all inventors (new or old) will not lose thousands and thousands of dollars by falling victim to this SCAM.

Smith, born August 20, 1964 in Orange County, California to parents Rodney Raymond and Jacqueline Jean Smith, has two brothers, Robert and Christian, and three sisters, Sheri, Julie and Christy.

Smith has a bachelor of science degree and an engineering degree. Smith was educated at the University of Phoenix and Arizona State University. Smith, his wife Tamra and two sons, Brandon and Blake reside in Arizona.

Smith enjoys fishing, flying and volleyball.